GUIDANCE MONOGRAPH SERIES

SHELLEY C. STONE

BRUCE SHERTZER

Editors

GUIDANCE MONOGRAPH SERIES

The general purpose of Houghton Mifflin's Guidance Monograph Series is to provide high quality coverage of topics which are of abiding importance in contemporary counseling and guidance practice. In a rapidly expanding field of endeavor, change and innovation are inevitably present. A trend accompanying such growth is greater and greater specialization. Specialization results in an increased demand for materials which reflect current modifications in guidance practice while simultaneously treating the field in greater depth and detail than commonly found in textbooks and brief journal articles.

The list of eminent contributors to this series assures the reader expert treatment of the areas covered. The monographs are designed for consumers with varying familiarity to the counseling and guidance field. The editors believe that the series will be useful to experienced practitioners as well as beginning students. While these groups may use the monographs with somewhat different goals in mind, both will benefit from the treatment given to content areas.

The content areas treated have been selected because of specific criteria. Among them are timeliness, practicality, and persistency of the issues involved. Above all, the editors have attempted to select topics which are of major substantive concern to counseling and guidance personnel.

Shelley C. Stone

Bruce Shertzer

CAREER

EDUCATION AND

HOME

ECONOMICS

CAROL A. CHRISTEN
RENSSELAER INDIANA
CENTRAL HIGH SCHOOL

HOUGHTON MIFFLIN COMPANY · BOSTON
ATLANTA · DALLAS · GENEVA, ILL. · HOPEWELL, N.J. · PALO ALTO

ISBN: 0–395–200504

Library of Congress Catalog Card
Number: 74–11977

CONTENTS

EDITORS' INTRODUCTION

Set IX of the Guidance Monograph Series is designed to treat the topic of career education and is intended for the use of teachers and counselors. The recent emphasis in educational circles on career education stresses that teachers are to have extensive input into the career education of their students from the elementary level through the secondary level. They are expected to draw out and teach the career implications of various subject matter areas. The contents of this set intentionally stress principles, procedures, techniques and materials of value to the classroom teacher in specific subject matter areas.

Dr. Christen's monograph focuses on career education in the home economics area. As a former teacher of home economics, school counselor and currently as a director of guidance she has brought together a resource for home economics teachers which will be of great value in implementing career education in the classroom. Her presentation provides a rich source of rationale, means of implementation and materials useful to those wishing to provide career education about careers both directly and indirectly related to home economics.

SHELLEY C. STONE
BRUCE SHERTZER

AUTHOR'S INTRODUCTION

This monograph is intended to help relate career education to the field of home economics and to the high school home economics teacher. Career education is not a new area of teaching, nor does it require a complete revision of the curriculum. Rather it is an additional way of relating subject matter to the world of work and to the student. What has been taught in the past can still be taught and, provided it is what the student can use, career education can enrich subject matter. Career education is not "something else" to do; it is another approach to what you, as a teacher, are now trying to do; namely, educate a student for the future so that both he and society can benefit. Work attitudes, work values, work techniques may be treated in career education, but fundamentally, career education depends upon what you do in the classroom to involve students in learning about the work world and how they might fit into it. No career decision has to be made, but at least students can become more planful about their entry into the work world. This monograph has been written for use by high school teachers. Therefore its content is related to units within the home economics field. There is overlap in that a foods teacher also may find useful ideas in the units on family living, consumer education, or general home economics.

There are countless ways to relate home economics to career education. The author has attempted to organize and present some ways that appear workable, but the teacher and the counselor working together will undoubtedly think of other very useful ideas. Communities and schools vary and, since both are most important to the career education concept, they must always be looked on as fundamental to the program. No matter how large or small the community or school, many resources are available for use in career education. Teachers and counselors must consider all available sources within their communities; it may be surprising how eager community members are to participate in the program. Just as there are many "people" resources, there are many commercial and homemade resources available. These resources are discussed in the chapter dealing with implementation as well as listed in appendices.

CAROL A. CHRISTEN

Home Economics: An Overview

History of Home Economics

One might be surprised to know that the home economics movement in the United States can be traced to a man! Sir Benjamin Thompson (Count Rumford), a British-American, was a noted heat-research scientist and founder of the Royal Institution. He directed his scientific interest and skill toward research and experimentation with kitchen ranges, fireplace designs, cooking utensils, food preparation and home heating and lighting in the late 1700s and early 1800s.

After Thompson, however, at the beginning of the 19th century, women came to the fore in the home economics field. The beginning of home economics training seems to be the needlework which was done by girls in the Boston public schools. In 1826 students in Mary Anna Longstreth's school were taught basic sewing, and young ladies in Emma Willard's female seminary were instructed in "housewifery." The young ladies took care of their own rooms, cared for their own clothes, and occasionally observed the pastry cook. While students at some women's colleges performed some domestic duties, it was really considered the duty of the mother to prepare daughters for homemaking.

The Morrill Land Grant Act of 1862 played an important part in the establishment of home economics as a field of study. That act provided each state a grant of land which was to be used for the founding of one or more colleges of agriculture and mechanics. When the Secretary of Agriculture in 1866 expressed the need for education to include home-related subjects, it seemed that the public had accepted home economics in education institutions.

While the land grant colleges were developing in the West, various schools, especially cooking schools, were emerging in the East. In 1863 the headmaster of the Winthrop School in Boston was persuaded by Mrs. Mary Hemenway to offer courses in cooking and sewing to girls. Mrs. Hemenway personally financed the Winthrop project as well as a school lunch program until the school officials assumed both.

Juliet Corson became the director of the Free Training School for Women in New York City in 1874 and later Miss Corson opened her own school. It was reported that between January and May of 1879 she taught 6,560 students! The Boston Cooking School, founded in 1879, was established as a training school for girls but later offered courses to anyone who wanted to take cooking classes. Other cooking schools appeared: the New Century Club in Philadelphia in 1878 and the Philadelphia School in 1881.

An early educator, Catherine E. Beecher, established two private schools for girls, one in Hartford, Connecticut in 1882 and one in Cincinnati, Ohio somewhat later. It was her belief that the teaching of "domestic economy" was needed, and she directed her efforts toward the writing of two books: *Treatise on Domestic Economy* and *Domestic Receipt Book.* The *Treatise,* in the first few chapters, dealt with woman's responsibilities as well as her social and national opportunities through home and school. An argument which justified the teaching of domestic economy as a subject was also presented.

Courses in domestic science appeared more and more frequently in the public schools between 1881 and 1890. Both the home economics courses in the land grant colleges and the cooking schools influenced growth in the number of courses offered by the public education system. This growth also was influenced by the parallel Manual Training Movement for boys, in that when mechanical drawing and industrial courses were offered to boys, sewing and domestic subjects were offered to girls. Sewing was taught in a Philadelphia high school and later extended into the elementary and grammar schools. In the New York City schools, sewing was introduced and a director of sewing was appointed. San Francisco began courses in domestic economy at about the same time. From east to west home economics had taken hold and an increasing demand for teachers qualified in the field emerged.

The Early 1900s

By 1907 eight colleges, located in the East, Midwest, and the West, had courses for training teachers in domestic science. In 1908 South Dakota State College offered a teacher training program. By the beginning of the 20th century the home economics movement had reached the point that there were recognized leaders in the field. A variety of activities paralleling formal education emerged at about the same time. Homemaking classes and other activities were sponsored by many civic organizations. Childrens' instruction in household activities through play resulted from the kitchen garden movement. An experiment to feed the poor scientifically resulted in the New England kitchen project. Although the project was unsuccessful, it predated the first school lunch program in Boston.

Home economics received attention at the Chicago World's Fair. The National Household Economic Association, the Rumford Kitchen, and the United States Department of Agriculture's collection and analysis of food materials were part of or emerged from the fair. The Rumford Kitchen, named in honor of Count Rumford, was originated by Mrs. Ellen Richards. The kitchen was part of an exhibit which showed a working man's home and attempted to demonstrate how his family could live on $500 a year. A part of the exhibit was a series of pamphlets written by authorities in several departments of science related to human food and nutrition. Because of her work in the New England Kitchen and the Rumford Kitchen, Mrs. Richards was invited to discuss the development of Regents examinations with Mr. Melvil Dewey, secretary of the New York State Board of Regents. Mrs. Richards was asked to discuss the content necessary for the household science examination. The Regents examinations were given for college entrance and household science was added to the examination program in 1896. In 1898 Mrs. Richards was asked to speak on domestic problems before several members of the Lake Placid Club in Lake Placid, New York. From this meeting there emerged a group of trained workers who met annually from 1899 to 1908. The Lake Placid Conferences formed a solid base for home economics and, because of their far reaching effects, each conference deserves separate mention.

The Lake Placid Conferences

The first conference looked at such 19th century changes as those created in the economy and economic functions due to industrialization; women's rights and restrictions imposed on women in education, professions, and politics; effects of increased leisure time for women and the accompanying formation of women's clubs; the contrast between the wealthy and the poor; the fact that goods-producing family members earned livelihoods away from home; and that families were predominately consumers rather than producers. The group considered "school at home and abroad, the college and university, the training of teachers and other leaders, source material including government bulletins, help for the homemaker, standards of living (especially as affected by sanitary science), domestic science in farmers' institute, and cooperation between agricultural experiment stations and domestic science schools [Baldwin, 1949, p. 12]." Perhaps one of the most enduring decisions made at the first conference was the choice of home economics as a title for the general area.

There were recommendations and resolutions generated at the conference. It was recommended that more United States Department of Agriculture bulletins be published and that schools and colleges keep in close contact with the Department and with experiment stations. One recommendation led to a resolution stating that since the public asked the state to recognize important sociologic problems of the home, state legislatures be asked to give the same attention to home economics as they give agriculture and mechanical arts in state schools and colleges. Several committees were created and charged to work on study courses, teacher training, housekeeping methods, mission work, kitchen garden classes, home economics library classification, program, and membership.

The second conference was held in 1900 and introduced the concept of home economics instruction in the grade schools. The aim as stated by Richards was "to develop in a child power to be used over his own environment, his food, clothing, and shelter [Baldwin, 1949, p. 13]." Also discussed were vacation and evening schools, extension work and hospital dietaries. The resolutions included a request to the National Education Association for the creation of a department of home economics to aid in the training of children for citizenship.

The 1901 conference was made up of people from various work settings such as public schools, colleges, hospitals, magazines, women's clubs, and the Department of Agriculture. A report of the courses of study included an outline which began in grade one (raffia mats and churning butter) through grade eight (study of food production, selection and preparation). The high school course included laundering, millinery, sewing, house structure, furnishings, first aid, and cooking.

The fourth conference treated less concrete topics, including the nature of family, the family's significance in the individual's development and society's development, ideals in future family life, economic functions of women, theories of prosperity, new-found leisure, social and industrial conditions. The conference gave a tentative definition of home economics: "Home economics, in its most comprehensive sense, is the study of the laws, conditions, principles, and ideals which are concerned on the one hand with man's immediate physical environment and on the other hand with his nature as a social being, and is the study especially of the relation between those two factors [Baldwin, 1949, p. 15]." In a narrower sense it was defined as the study of empirical sciences with reference to practical problems of housework, cooking and the like. The complete definition would have included the philosophical basis for the subject — its relation to economics, sociology, chemistry, hygiene and other fields of study.

While the fifth conference dealt primarily with the labor problems of household and institutional employees, the sixth looked at ways to incorporate home economics into education. Many of the problems were not so very different from today perhaps, since in one address to the conference, Mrs. Richards said, "the disintegration of the family is seen in separation of wage earning brothers and sisters who no longer feel constrained to live together under one roof, each boards with companions more congenial. The aged parent is often settled in an apartment with a paid companion. The children have their own separate rooms and playhouses, are sent away to summer camps and on school trips to herd with their own kind instead of adding either pleasure or profit to the parent's life [Baldwin, 1949, pp. 17–18]." The best name for the education branch was discussed and among the choices were domestic science, domestic economy, household economics, household administration, and euthenics. This latter word was defined to mean the science of controllable environment and many thought it to be the best choice.

The last four conferences reviewed and renewed facts from previous ones. The seventh conference in 1904 presented the expansion of home economics education. The South seemed to be doing very little, the East a bit more, and the West was devoted to legislation that would provide money to enlarge the field. Teachers who reported on home economics at the ninth conference presented the following facts: in Houston, Texas, all teachers were encouraged to relate their work to home economics; in Toledo, Ohio, high school girls' manual training (home economics) classes were placed on the same level as other subjects; and, those states that required home economics teachers to have degrees commanded greater respect for their departments than those who did not. When the organization committee recommended that a national group be formed to carry on the ideas of the conferences, the teaching section of the Lake Placid conference met in December of 1908 to form the American Home Economics Association.

The AHEA

The American Home Economics Association provided leadership in many ways. By 1911 the membership had reached 1,078 and home economics was firmly established in the schools. In the decade that followed, home economics education had incorporated child care, classes for boys, housing and money management into its program. As other scientific and educational groups gave recognition to home economics, there was within the AHEA an increasing emphasis placed on economics and social sciences rather than the natural sciences. World War I demanded that attention be given to conservation and emergency measures.

Expansion of Home Economics Education

The Smith-Hughes Act of 1917 was passed and provided impetus to vocational training in agriculture, the trades, industry and homemaking. Attention in home economics was given not only to the education and needs of homemakers during school years but also extended to programs for adults. This added dimension supported the extension program which had been originated with the passage of the Smith-Levee Act in 1914. The Cooperative Agriculture Extension Service was designed to help educate adults for better living and contributed greatly to the home economics field. Some concerns, however, were voiced by professionals in the field. These concerns were that work with the hands was termed manual even though science was applied in it, as compared to work from a book which was termed cultural and therefore enjoyed higher social status. The removal of this stigma was viewed as an opportunity for home economists!

The American Home Economics Association has been the major guiding force in American home economics education. About 3,000 high schools had home economics departments in 1916 and this number increased to more than 8,000 by 1921. Schools in general asked students to select one of four curricula or program options: trade, business, liberal arts, or home economics and to remain within that area throughout secondary school. However, because most female students eventually became homemakers, many schools encouraged electives to be taken in the home economics department. Between 1910 and 1928 the number of students enrolled in high school home economics classes increased by 1,229 percent! While home economics was usually a requirement at the junior high school level, it sometimes was included in the elementary grades. In the elementary school, especially, teachers attempted to show children the relationship of food to health.

By 1928 the original home economics courses of cooking, sewing, millinery had expanded in many states to include child care, family and community relations, and home management. Nursery schools were being established; the first one connected to a public school system was started in 1924 in Highland Park, Michigan. Early home economics leaders such as Isabel Bevier and Helen Atwater considered home economics responsible for teaching sane living, good citizenship, the joy of work, and healthy family relationships. It was necessary to make "people realize the relation of the individual to the family and of the family to the community together with the economic, social, and moral impact of those relations [Baldwin, 1949, pp. 78–79]." Other leaders, Katherine Blunt and Margaret Justin, rejoiced in the work of child care and development. Miss Justin felt that the society's economic reorganization had lessened the need for children to work in the home, therefore the family faced the problem of children as economic liabilities rather than as partial assets. Lita Bane felt home economics should incorporate psychology as an aid in solving behavior problems in homes as well as mental hygiene and family adjustment problems.

In the period of 1929–34 various independent studies and government statistical studies were conducted. A result of one of these studies showed that the teaching of family relationships was favored, but certain areas such as "companionate marriage and declining birth rate" were questioned. A survey showed that 35 percent of the junior high schools and 68 percent of senior high schools offered classes in family relationships. Seven thousand boys were participating in home economics classes and the request for these classes often came from the boys themselves. A White House conference stimulated child care courses in elementary, junior and senior high schools. The greatest interest in the area was found in the eighth and twelfth grades. Consumer education was making its debut into the home economics curriculum. Ninety percent of the city high schools and 54 percent of rural high schools offered home economics classes.

The Emergency Act of 1933, designed to ease unemployment, provided adult education in home economics and vocational training at the secondary school level. However, many high school home economics classes were dropped during the depression years. An interesting survey reported during this time asked fourteen different groups of superintendents, principals, deans, and supervising teachers to rate six high school subjects and six extracurricular activities in order of their contribution toward the seven cardinal principles of education. The results showed home economics rated first, which hardly justified its being classified a frill!

Funds of $1 million were provided by the 1934 George-Ellzey Act. These funds were for vocational education in high schools for three years. At the end of this time the George-Dean Act authorized the use of $4 million for vocational education for the salaries and travel of teachers and supervisors employed in adult education. States were required to have a five year plan in order to receive this federal aid which, no doubt, gave a firm boost to home economics education. By the end of the thirties, 90 percent of city schools, 65 percent of village schools, and 57 percent of rural schools offered home economics. Sixty-five percent of female high school graduates had taken home economics courses. Still another important recognition of the home economics field was the appointment of Dr. Muriel W. Brown as consultant in family life education in the Home Economics Education Service of the United States Office of Education in 1940.

The 1963 Vocational Education Act attempted to meet present and future needs of vocational education. The earlier acts had helped education prepare students for becoming housewives but did nothing to prepare students for non-college home economics-related careers. The 1963 Act allotted funds to prepare students for occupations in child care, nursing homes, hospitals, food service and garment manufacturing.

The 1968 Amendments to the Act provided funds intended mainly to develop programs for the disadvantaged. The Act stipulated that one-third of the funds be used in programs to assist consumers and to help improve home environments and quality of family life in economically depressed areas or in areas of high rates of unemployment. Further, fifteen percent of those benefitted by funds must be disadvantaged, 10 percent handicapped, and 15 percent enrolled in post high school education. In order to be funded, programs were required to: 1) encourage consideration of social and cultural conditions and needs; 2) offer career opportunities at all levels of home economics and consumer education; 3) encourage preparation for professional leadership; 4) stress employability by including such subjects as personal relations and grooming; offer consumer education as an integral part of the curriculum; and 5) educate for the dual role of wage earner and homemaker.

The home economics field will grow and progress from this legislation. It is probable that even greater emphasis will be seen in vocational training, consumer education, and family life. The growth of the field in the last sixty years speaks for its reason for being.

Curricular Areas of Home Economics

Although the curriculum in departments of home economics may differ, most will include some or all of the following areas: foods, clothing, child development, family living, housing, and consumer education. Within these areas various kinds of units may be included, with each teacher including those areas seen as most beneficial to the students.

The foods unit may start with basics and progress to specialities; it can range from learning how to measure ingredients to preparing gourmet meals. Elements of good nutrition and meal planning incorporated into wise food selection and buying may be part of the unit. Techniques of food preparation, attractive ways of serving food, table setting, and manners will be included in the material presented. Selection of china, silver, and crystal may be incorporated. Recently food preservation has been revived in light of the rising cost of food as well as the current interest in natural foods.

The revival of needlecraft has been seen in the clothing area, where such crafts as needlepoint, crewel and thread embroidery, quilting, knitting, and crocheting are taught. Of course, garment construction, from the simple skirt to the tailored project, are the basis of the clothing unit. Somewhere in the clothing unit, pattern selection, design and style, and wardrobe planning will appear, as will understanding and knowledge about fiber content and the care of different fibers and the fabrics made from these fibers. Grooming units are often included in this area because personal appearance fits well into its context. When a laundering unit is included in the curriculum, it is often part of the clothing area.

As subject areas evolved, child care and development was added to the curriculum. Child development may involve learning about life from conception to pre-adolescence. A babysitting unit is often included because it is so pertinent, especially in the early high school years. In addition to physical, social, and pyschological growth of children, selection and purchase of clothing and toys may also be studied. Units may also deal with the relationship of food and nutrition to body growth and development and the selection and use of children's games and literature.

The family-living class usually includes topics such as dating, courtship, engagement, marriage, and family relationships. A realistic look at the financial costs found in family living is taken by presenting the expenses of marriage, housing, illness, birth, and death. Budgets for different income levels may be covered as well as related housing decisions. Business factors such as wills, contracts, and money management may be covered. Divorce and the problems related to it are discussed, as well as such subjects as abortion and drugs.

Housing units generally cover different kinds of housing such as houses, apartments, mobile homes and ways of decorating each. Furniture and appliances appropriate for different homes may be studied along with their selection and care. Down payments, mortgages, problems and decisions involved in home buying are also usually included in housing units.

Although consumer education is sometimes taught in other subject areas (e.g., economics courses), it is a natural area of concern for the home economics department. Consumer education is often included in units on food, clothing, family living and housing. Knowing how, what, and when to buy cannot be overstressed in any of these areas. Consumer education will often include banking, savings, investments, loans, stocks, budgets, retail and wholesale buying and advertising.

Recently high school curricula have begun to offer more male-oriented classes such as boys' foods class, family relations, and consumer education. Sometimes the boys' home economics classes are called bachelor living or bachelor survival. These courses are focused on the boys' needs, and may include units on foods, which teach basic cooking skills; clothing, which teach the use of the sewing machine for making and mending garments; housing units, which stress information about apartments, rooms, houses and the furnishing of each; and consumer education which teach related business operations.

Home Economics and the World of Work

The concept of relating careers to subject matter is not new to most home economics teachers. Home economics has historically been "work-oriented." Perhaps this is true because home economics has traditionally felt its relationship to many different work areas and especially to homemaking. Homemaking involves many skills — the homemaker usually must be a cook, maid, business person, chauffeur, seamstress, child psychologist, nutritionist, ad infinitum. Perhaps this is why home economics has trained women for so many different jobs. Although boys have been included in home economics classes, the majority of time and effort has been spent to provide experiences that would be useful for girls to use as they assume their adult role. In recent years, especially with the womens' lib movement, home economics has attempted to relate the many talents it develops to careers other than those used in the home. Indeed these areas are many: education, community service, communication and media, dietetics, food service, and business. Home economics teachers are fortunate in that their subject matter lends itself quite naturally to many parts of the work world.

The outlook for service-producing industries in the coming decade shows great growth, much greater than for goods-producing industries. It is projected that some 21 million workers will be employed in service-producing industries in 1980 — up from 15 million in 1968. These are the industries that will use many home economics-related workers. Service-producing industries include government, transportation, communications, public utilities, wholesale and retail trade, finance, insurance, real estate, and food, health, personal, and educational services.

Predictions indicate that white collar jobs will outnumber blue-collar jobs in 1980 but blue-collar jobs will increase by 2 million workers between 1970 and 1980. Within the white collar group several of the professional and technical occupations will grow more rapidly. Among those that relate to home economics are urban planners, recreation, social, and health workers, sales workers, managers, and a variety of other service jobs.

The number and proportion of women in the work force will continue to increase. One of the important by-products of this trend will undoubtedly be a need for more day care centers. This raises a number of issues in home economics: effectively relating work to women, and providing trained day care center personnel. Still another dimension will have to be dealt with: educating youth to cope with the combination of marriage, child-rearing, and work.

Although traditionally female oriented, home economics is offering more and more opportunities for men. Boys, too, need to know about home economics-related careers. Jobs in child care centers, nursery schools, kindergartens, and elementary schools are growing demand areas for males. Men who have home economics backgrounds are employed in corporate business, decorating, retail business, home furnishing, university teaching, family economics, human development, nutrition, housing, merchandising, and food services.

Home economists are primarily people-oriented and should be concerned about people and their needs. Depending upon the home economist's work setting, specific qualities are necessary. For example, the teacher must enjoy working with young people and be willing to hear and discuss their feelings and needs. The extension worker must feel comfortable with people of different ages and with people from different social backgrounds. Leadership ability is important in this area, also. In business the home economist may need skill in communication, in organizing, and in delegating responsibility. In research the home economist needs to be accurate, systematic, imaginative, patient, perceptive. Most home economists need to be sensitive, objective and accepting of different values and life styles.

2

Careers Directly Related
To Home Economics

Often it is difficult to decide whether a specific job is directly or indirectly related to home economics. This chapter presents the author's division of job areas, briefly describes the job, and lists the level of education or training needed. There are many excellent sources useful in obtaining more detailed information about a specific job. Information concerning the nature of the work, personal characteristics, interests, abilities, training possibilities, places of employment, earnings, and outlook for the future are usually given in such sources. These sources are given in appendices A and B. The *Dictionary of Occupational Titles* code is included for all the jobs listed in this and the following chapter which have the *DOT* code.

Foods

Waitress, Waiter (DOT Code 311.878), Host, Hostess (DOT Code 310.868)

Employment can be found in a variety of settings, from the local drive-in to the fanciest restaurant in town. On-the-job training is available and rather easily obtained. All jobs involve dealing with people, both in serving patrons and with co-workers. Waitresses and waiters take orders, serve food, usually clear the table, compute the bill. The hostess greets and seats patrons. She may serve coffee when she presents the menu.

Dish Carrier — Busboy, Busgirl (DOT Code 311.878)

Employment, as with waiters and waitresses, is found in a variety of settings. A dish carrier works in dining areas carrying food for the waiter or waitress to serve, clearing tables and taking dirty dishes to the kitchen. There is indirect work with patrons. On-the-job training is available and some dish carriers will move into other jobs of more responsibility, such as waiter or waitress.

Food Processing Worker (DOT Code 529.886) or Technician (DOT Code 022.281, 029.381)

Line workers in canneries or plants need a minimum of training and are trained on the job. There is little contact with people except with co-workers. Work tends to be routine.

Technicians work in several different areas such as assisting research scientists in development and quality control of food processing. They may also work in the production end in such areas as packaging, processing, and sanitation. Special training programs are offered in community colleges or other post-secondary schools. Such programs are usually two years in length.

Food Service Worker (DOT Code 313.381)

This area includes a great variety of jobs that can be found in cafeterias, restaurants, nursing homes, hospitals, schools, and dormitories. In most settings it would be necessary to work congenially with co-workers. Preparation varies and can include on-the-job training, one- or two-year post-secondary training programs, or, in the case of a gourmet chef, many years of formal training and experience. In each setting there will be a manager or director who may or may not have a college degree. Certainly knowledge of institutional management is necessary and can be obtained either through training or experience. Working under the manager there may be several cooks, chefs, pantry workers, etc., depending upon the size of the operation.

Cooks' and chefs' responsibilities vary from setting to setting. They prepare food, usually in large quantities. Chefs often specialize in the preparation of one kind of food or perhaps in one method of cooking. They also may be in charge of the kitchen. Cooks may receive training in vocational or trade schools as well as on the job. Cooks and chefs often serve an apprenticeship after formal training is completed. Apprenticeships are offered by trade unions and by large hotels and restaurants and usually are two or three years in length. Other training programs vary over time from a few months to two years or longer.

Cooks in institutions such as hospitals, schools, nursing homes, and dormitories prepare food in large quantities, usually somewhat less creatively than their counterparts in commercial establishments. Because food budgets are somewhat restrictive in institutions, cooks in these settings prepare tasty, nutritious food that is also economical.

Pantry workers prepare special kinds of food such as salads and desserts. On-the-job training may be given although a one-year training program may be of help in securing a job.

Baker (DOT Code 526.781)

Bakers may work in the kitchen of a restaurant, in a large baking company or in their own business. There are obvious differences in talents that may be needed in different settings. The baker in a restaurant will prepare breads, pastries, and desserts for the day's menu. The baker in a large commercial company will bake large quantities of bread, rolls, coffee cake, etc. The baker in a retail shop will prepare a large variety of goods each day, and probably will need additional skills in business, especially if he owns the shop. Bakers receive training in an apprentice program which lasts two to four years.

Food Salesperson (DOT Code 290.877)

The over-the-counter salespersons, vendors, route salespersons, retail salespersons, and food checkers all fall into the food sales occupation category. There are many food products and food related products sold. People in sales who enjoy their work are person-oriented and are in contact with people constantly. Some salespersons work directly with foods, such as over-the-counter sales. Others work for large companies that have several food products to sell (e.g., General Mills, General Foods, Pet Milk, Kraft). The over-the-counter salesperson and the food checker need less training than the company salesperson. The company salesperson usually has post secondary training which may be obtained on the job or through two- to four-year college program.

Nutritionist (DOT Code 077.128)

Employed by the government, companies, hospitals, and research centers, nutritionists examine food processes of the body and the uses of essential nutrients by the body. Nutritionists are college graduates with extensive graduate work.

Dietitian (DOT Code 077.128)

Dietitians plan menus and diets to provide proper nutrition to individuals and groups. They are employed in a variety of places:

hospitals, clinics, public eating places, private cafeterias for companies or factories, the military, or universities which offer courses of study in home economics, dietetics, dentistry, medicine, nursing, or allied health fields. Dietitians receive their training in a four-year college program. A one-year internship or three years experience is needed to gain full professional standing.

Food Technologist and Food Scientist (DOT Code 096.128)

These people work in industry, government, research, and educational institutions in many capacities. Their work may entail developing improved foods, conducting research on food processes, inspecting the quality of foods, or designing packaging techniques. At least four years of college training in the food sciences is required.

Positions in Business and Utility Companies

Home economists are employed also in test kitchens of industries and by utility companies. The duties may be varied: they may develop new recipes, new products and new ways to use products; they may design and prepare food displays or food photography for advertising; they may demonstrate the proper way to use a new piece of kitchen equipment. A bachelor's degree or a master's degree is necessary.

Clothing

There are numerous careers in the designing, cutting and sewing areas of the apparel industry.

Patternmaker and Pattern Grader (DOT Code 781.381)

The patternmaker constructs the full-size master pattern. Using the designer's sketch or sample garment, the patternmaker creates the paper pattern pieces. Training is usually acquired through years of experience on the job. Sometimes pattern graders, those who translate the pattern into many sizes, advance to patternmaker. Pattern graders usually gain training in the cutting room or in other related jobs and are trained on the job.

Marker (DOT Code 781.484) and Cutter (DOT Code 781.884)

The Occupational Outlook Handbook lists five basic operations for the cutting department: spreading, marking, cutting, assembly, and ticketing. Hand or machine spreaders lay the material out into exact lengths on the cutting board. Markers place pattern pieces so that the greatest number of pieces can be cut from the material. Cutters are the people who cut the various pieces from the layers of material which have been marked on the spread out material. Assemblers collect, bundle, and mark garment pieces and add the needed lining, tape, and trimming for the complete garment. The material is then sent to the sewing room. For the most part skills in these areas are learned on the job, although some plants do offer four-year apprentice programs. Most workers start as assemblers and work their way to spreader, marker, cutter. Several years of experience are needed.

Sewing Machine Operator (DOT Code 787.885)

Using machines that are heavier and faster than those found in homes, sewing machine operators in industry specialize in one operation such as attaching cuffs, sewing side seams. While some previous experience is preferred, many operators start in industries that require no experience and acquire their skill through on-the-job training.

Dressmaker (DOT Code 785.361) and Tailor (DOT Code 787.261)

Dressmakers and tailors construct garments from start to finish. Both machine and hand sewing is done. They must also be able to correctly fit garments. Vocational schools offer training for dressmaking and tailoring. Such training is essential to the work.

Alterations or Repair Tailor/Seamstress (DOT Code 785.281, 785.381)

Two related dressmaking jobs are those of alterations and repair and mending. People engaged in these jobs alter garments to fit the individual as well as repair and mend garments that have been damaged. Many of these individuals are self-employed and others are employed by retail stores. Part-time work is possible in this field. Training and experience are needed, although a high school education is usually sufficient.

Apparel Presser (DOT Code 363.884, 363.782)

Pressers use various types of pressing equipment to assure shape and appearance of garment. On-the-job training is necessary and such training is usually short-term. Employment can be found in industry, stores and cleaning shops.

Drapery Maker (DOT Code 299.488, 299.381, 787.885)

Employed by interior designers, furniture stores, retail stores, or self-employed, drapery makers are trained to make many sizes and kinds of drapes. Training may be obtained in tailoring courses or through on-the-job training.

Fabric Salesperson (DOT Code 263.458)

Understanding of fibers and fabrics enables this type of salesperson to help a customer select fabric. Thread, zipper, buttons and other notions must also be selected for most garments. Being knowledgeable about laundering techniques and care of fabric is helpful also. On-the-job training is given and high school or vocational school training may be useful.

Fabric Designer (DOT Code 142.081)

Creating different fabric designs using new and old fibers and artistic talent, the fabric designer is both artist and designer. The fabric designer must be knowledgeable about the properties of each fiber in the fabric and about fashion trends. A college degree is desirable although experience and on-the-job training may be substituted.

Textile Technician (DOT Code 029.381)

Textile technicians work in the laboratory doing routine kinds of testing such as determining tensile strength and creaseability of fabrics. They may also conduct research on new fibers and fabrics. Technicians may work under a scientist in the lab. Post-high school training, usually two to four years, is required for this work.

Fashion and Fabric Coordinator (DOT Code 185.158)

Employed by stores, retail clothing companies and magazines, fashion coordinators choose colors, fabrics and clothes for displays or illustrations. They may work with fashion shows or fashion information centers. While college training is preferred, two or three years of fashion or art education in a trade school, an art school, or a community college may be sufficient.

Company Representative (DOT Code 293.358)

Employed by sewing machine, pattern, thread, zipper or other notion-producing companies, company representatives demonstrate the company's products to the consumers and prospective retail buyers. Many representatives work with home economics teachers to demonstrate the company's equipment and products to the students in classes. A college degree is helpful.

Buyer (DOT Code 162.158)

Buyers are employed mainly to stock stores with products. They must, therefore, be knowledgeable about business trends and consumer needs. They may also work with advertising and sales personnel. A college degree is usually needed as well as some experience in the field.

Fashion Designer (DOT Code 142.081)

Creating and sketching the design for garments is the main job of fashion designers. They may drape, fit, and make sample pattern and garments. Usually they choose colors and fabrics and estimate the cost of garments. A college degree and years of experience are needed for success in the field. Some designers have two or three years of other training such as that received in trade or art school or junior college.

Display Designer (DOT Code 142.081)

Like garment designers, display designers specialize in creating attractive ways to show garments or fabrics. They may work in a retail store or for a magazine. College or art school training is usually preferred, however, on-the-job training may be substituted.

Fashion Illustrator (DOT Code 141.081)

Illustrators use creative and artistic talent to sketch or draw garments for pattern companies, fashion magazines, or newspapers. Training is often received in a two- or three-year art school program.

Child Development

Babysitter (DOT Code 307.878)

Babysitters are employed many different places. Duties vary depending upon place of employment. Some babysitters are only employed part-time and various duties, such as entertainment and care of children, preparation of meals, and light housework may be included.

Other babysitters work full-time and their duties may be more comprehensive and include not only care of children but also care of clothes, food and the household. No formal training is necessary although high school classes in child care and experience are good preparation.

Foster Parent (DOT Code 309.878)

Foster parents care for children who are wards of the court. They provide all the care and deal with all the responsibilities that natural parents might. No formal training is necessary, however homes must be approved by social or welfare agencies in order to assure that children will be properly cared for.

4-H Leader (DOT Code 096.128)

4-H leaders are volunteer leaders for boys and girls in 4-H Clubs. They work with young people on various projects dealing with food, clothing, home furnishings, crafts, gardening and agriculture. Training is required only as it is needed to teach specific skills. Extension services also have youth agents who work with 4-H leaders and directly with youth in 4-H programs. Youth agents are college educated and hold at least an undergraduate degree.

Head-Start Worker

Head-Start workers include administrators, teachers, and aides. Head-Start programs provide learning experiences for preschool children from disadvantaged areas. Administrators and teachers are trained in education and usually have bachelor's or master's degrees. Aides may have one or two years of college training but some have years of experience and no post-secondary education.

Youth Group Leader

Girl and Boy Scouts, Campfire Girls, YMCA, YWCA, and Christian Education programs employ people to direct and operate programs for children of various ages. Many kinds of skills and crafts are taught. While the director usually has college training and special preparation in recreation, the workers may need only interest, skill, and an ability to teach in areas such as crafts, cooking, tailoring, etc.

Day Care Center Worker (DOT Code 359.878)

Day care centers care for and provide recreational and educational services to young children of working mothers. The director usually must have college training. Workers in the center may include a cook who prepares and serves meals as well as teachers who care for and play with the children who may be in their care from morning to late afternoon. Some training is helpful for workers and some community colleges offer one- or two-year programs in child care.

Extension Specialist in Child Development (DOT Code 096.168)

The extension specialist in child development travels throughout a state helping other extension service workers and working with the public in areas of child care and child development. Speaking to groups, conducting workshops, and working with small groups on problems of child care may be part of the job. An undergraduate degree is needed and a master's degree may be required since this person serves as a resource person for special problems.

Nursery School Teacher (DOT Code 359.878)

The nursery school is usually attended by 4–5 year old children. Teachers in this field provide supervised learning experiences; they tell stories, play games, sing songs. Teachers are required to have a high school education as a minimum. Some states may require a teacher's certificate, and if so a college degree is required.

Kindergarten Teacher (DOT Code 092.228)

The kindergarten teacher provides supervised learning experiences for young children. Social skills and attitudes are introduced as are language, number, health, and safety concepts. College training is required for state certification as a teacher.

Family Relationships

Visiting Homemaker and Aide

Employed by private agencies or by publicly supported services such as Family Services, a visiting homemaker contacts people who need special help, evaluates the particular situation, and determines the best way to provide such services. For example, an elderly person may need part-time assistance in caring for the home and an aide could fill that need. Meals may need to be furnished and the homemaker may make arrangement for meals to be brought to the home by volunteer organizations who usually cooperate with hospital kitchens. Sometimes the person only needs an occasional visit to make sure all is well. The visiting homemaker also may help with related family problems such as financial, marital, or housing problems and make referrals to other helping agencies. A college degree is required for the visiting homemaker but aides may have only a high school education.

Shopping Consultant (DOT Code 296.358)

Shopping consultants are usually employed by large department stores to help customers in purchasing. Problems such as size selection and gift selections may be referred to the shopping consultant. Call-in or mail-in orders for personal shopping may be referred also. If customers are unsure of what to purchase, they may confer with the shopping consultant before actually making the purchase. A broad background is needed to successfully help customers. College education is often required although years of experience could be substituted.

Educational and Consumer Relations Worker (DOT Code 204.388)

Informing customers and the public about products is the job of people involved in educational and consumer relations. Many companies employ people to act as resources for teachers. As new products are purchased, the best ways to use them is demonstrated. Many of these people are employed by government or private agencies to study products and then relate the information to the public. College training is required for most jobs.

Home Management Specialist

Home management specialists investigate ways to run homes more efficiently and relate this information to the homemaker. They may do this through educational programs offered by companies or through articles in magazines and newspapers. A college education is required for the job.

Case Work (DOT Code 195.108)

The case workers work in welfare offices or for private agencies gathering information concerning families or persons. Their job involves interviewing people, seeking information, and then synthesizing the information into a formal report to provide some recommendation for action. Case workers are involved with people who have various kinds of problems and need help from outside sources. Case workers are usually college trained.

Nutritionist and Aide (DOT Code 077.128, 319.138)

Nutritionists are employed by industry or by government agencies, usually to research food and food uses by families or to educate families or groups on food and food uses. Many are employed in urban areas where there are large numbers of disadvantaged families who need help in wise food buying and in nutritious food preparation as well as education for understanding nutritional needs of the body. Nutritionists are college educated with at least a bachelor's degree. The nutritionist aide works with families by going into the home and showing homemakers techniques to use in food preparation. Aides have high school education and some additional training.

Extension Specialist in Family Relations (DOT Code 096.168)

Employed by the Cooperative Extension Service, specialists in family relations travel within a state to work with other extension workers, 4-H leaders, and community members in various areas of family living. They may conduct workshops in human relationships, discuss family problems (child-parent, wife-husband, child-child), or train people to conduct workshops and discussions. Their speciality in family relations demands a college degree and graduate work in the field.

Family Financial Counselor (DOT Code 189.158)

Financial counselors work in many different settings dealing with family financial concerns. They may work in banks, finance companies or departments, and insurance companies. Investment in insurance, bonds, or stocks, savings, down payments on homes, monthly mortgage payments, car payments, credit buying all may be reasons for a family to consult a financial counselor. Because counselors are aware of economic realities and their implications, they are able to suggest ways in which a family can best use its income. Financial counseling usually requires a college degree.

Family Counselor (DOT Code 195.108)

The family counselor works with couples who have marital problems, children who have problems with parents and/or siblings, etc. Many kinds of specific problems may be involved — family interrelationships, educational and social difficulties, and financial concerns. Sometimes family members are worked with individually; other times several or all the family members are seen together. The family counselor must have at least a master's degree in order to be certified.

Housing

Buyer (DOT Code 162.158)

Furniture buyers are employed by furniture and department stores to select and purchase wholesale furniture. Buyers are required to understand needs of customers, develop a sales approach and maintain a well-balanced stock of furniture. They must be knowledgeable about different kinds of furniture and furniture construction. A high school education may be sufficient but a college degree will be an advantage to the beginner.

Furniture Designer (DOT Code 142.081)

As with other designers, furniture designers create pieces of furniture for manufacture. A knowledge of design trends, costs, production capabilities, and the sales market is necessary. Designers must have artistic talent in relating line, comfort, and beauty. An understanding of upholstery fabrics and their capabilities is important as is knowledge of woods or metals. Post-secondary education is needed, which might consist of 2–4 years of art school, community college or undergraduate college work.

Interior Decorator or Designer (DOT Code 142.051)

The interior decorator or designer plans artistic interiors of homes and business offices. Planning the room decor, including furniture selection, draperies, floor coverings and accessories are part of the decorator's service. The decorator must know about costs of materials and something about the customer's personality and life style in order to achieve pleasing and satisfactory results. Two to three years in an art or design institute or a 4-year undergraduate program is necessary. Sometimes on-the-job training is required also.

Home Service Director (DOT Code 096.168)

The director for home services directs consumer education services for companies by planning and coordinating consumer and research programs. Consumer programs include interpreting consumer habits and preferences and devising programs to educate the consumer in the use of the product. Employment is available in various settings such as equipment and food industries or public utilities. A college education is necessary.

Home Service Representative (DOT Code 278.258)

Employed by utility companies, home service representatives demonstrate equipment and appliances. The demonstrations may be used to promote sales or to educate homemakers in the most efficient use of equipment. The home service representative may visit the home to demonstrate and/or resolve problems involving appliances such as stoves, washers, and dryers. The representative also explains the use, care, and operation of equipment to schools and dealers. An undergraduate degree is required.

Household Products Salesperson (DOT Code 260.–206.458), Researcher (DOT Code 189.118), Technician (DOT Code .002–.029)

Several areas related to household products in which a person may work are sales, research, and technology. All involve dealing with products such as cleaning compounds, waxes, air purifiers, and paper products. The researcher and technician work in development and perfection of the product, and the salesperson in selling the product to the public. Education for the researcher and technician varies from graduate work (research) to 2–4 years undergraduate work (technician). Sales people may or may not have postsecondary training.

Equipment Development Occupations

Although the actual design of a piece of equipment may be done by an engineer, the home economist can play an important part in describing and perfecting it. People involved in equipment development study consumer complaints, problems, and suggestions and then attempt to design equipment accordingly. Sometimes new equipment is produced as a result of the study, other times improvements are made on existing equipment. A college education is necessary for this work.

Equipment Salesperson (DOT Code 278.358)

Another area in which salespersons are employed is the area of equipment sales. As in many selling jobs the equipment salesperson sells the product to the dealer or to the customer directly. A knowledgeable salesperson knows the features of the equipment that make it attractive, functional, and economical. Many sales people serve as resources for designers. Some training beyond high school is helpful.

Building and Remodeling Consultant

Consultants employed by contractors and sometimes large lumber yards work with customers who are contemplating building new homes or remodeling old structures. They discuss house plans and may assist with financial planning and decorating. Consultants will provide the client with information about building materials, paints, wallpaper, finishes, wiring, plumbing. A college education is needed.

Mobile Homes — Related Occupations

Some discussion should be directed toward jobs in the growing mobile home industry. These are various jobs in the area, such as design, sales, production, and furnishing. Home economists are used in designing the structure, the furniture, and the equipment as well as in decorating and advertising. A college education is necessary for these jobs.

Extension Specialist in Housing (DOT Code 096.128)

The extension specialist in housing works with other extension leaders in planning, developing, organizing, and evaluating programs related to housing. Extension specialists are well versed in all areas: building, finishing, furnishing, financing, decorating, lighting. A bachelor's degree is necessary and graduate work is preferred.

Government Positions (DOT Code 096.)

The federal government employs people to work with housing projects and with housing services in general. Much of the time these people are involved in research or communications concerning housing problems such as finances, materials, and living patterns. A college education is necessary.

Housekeeping Services — Executive (DOT Code 187.168), Housekeeper (DOT Code 321.138), Maid/Butler (DOT Code 323.887)

Several jobs are included in the general area of housekeeping. An executive housekeeper is responsible for directing the housekeeping program in institutions such as hospitals, hotels, motels, retirement centers, and dormitories. That responsibility involves establishing standards and procedures for work and supervising the work of others. Monitoring of supplies, records, budgets, repairs, and improvements may be included in the duties. A college education is recommended but some of the necessary training may be obtained through short courses offered at community colleges. In addition to the executive housekeeper, there are housekeeping workers who clean rooms and hallways, make up beds, replenish paper supplies and glasses etc. On-the-job training is usually given. Some housekeeping duties are performed by individuals or small independent companies who provide housecleaning services to private individuals. These people usually work in private homes on a weekly basis. Training is usually received on the job.

Consumer Education

Marketing Specialist (DOT Code 050.088)

Marketing specialists work as researchers studying the condition of their product's market. They determine potential sales, analyze data on past and present sales, collect data on competitive products, analyze buyers' habits and preferences, and study the national and world economy in general. College education is necessary.

Consumer Advisor (DOT Code 096.128)

Consumer service is offered by many companies. Consumer advisors work in development and sales of products. They may demonstrate products, lecture, develop consumer programs, suggest improvements in products based on customer reaction, or prepare material for customers. Some food chains employ a consumer advisor to work with customers' problems related to the buying and preparation of food. These people have a college degree.

Consultant

Consultants are employed in many different settings — industries of all kinds, public utilities, banks, stores, school systems, hospitals. Their job is to relate public interests and needs to the employer and provide public service. College training is necessary.

General

There are some areas of home economics that do not fit clearly and exclusively in a specific area and will be discussed under the general heading.

Homemaker

Homemaking consists of a myriad of jobs. Jobs related to all the areas of home economics are included. Homemaking is as varied as the many homemakers we have; it is a full time job for some and a part-time job for others. It may involve a large or small family, a large or small house, a large or small budget. A personal priority of homemaking duties is developed by each homemaker and this priority reflects the personal philosophy of the homemaker. There is no specialized training except that received in homes and school prior to establishment of the new home.

Teacher (DOT Code 091.228)

The teacher instructs students in the areas of foods, clothing, child development, family relations, housing, and consumer education. Time is spent in planning and preparing daily lessons and in direct contact instructing students. More time is spent in demonstrating, in showing, and in supervising students' activities than in lecture. Teachers work with different age students. A bachelor's degree is required. State certification is required for employment in the public schools. In many states a master's degree must be earned within a specific time to retain teacher certification.

Home Economics Extension Specialist (DOT Code 096.128)

Specialists in the field of home economics extension work have been discussed earlier. However, there is an extension person who works not as a specialist but more as a generalist in home economics. This person is involved with people in a specific geographical area and deals with media, the 4-H, women's clubs, welfare agencies. College training is required.

Welfare Worker (DOT Code 195.108, 195.168)

People employed by public welfare departments administer the county, city or state program which includes welfare claims, public assistance, court wards, food stamps, etc. Counseling in the areas of family finance, housing, etc., is often part of the job. While those who are employed in cities may specialize in specific kinds of problems, those in small towns or rural areas must be prepared to deal with a great variety of problems. College training is required for directors and case workers.

Communications Occupations

Home economists who desire to work in communications may find employment in various media, such as television, newspapers, radio, or magazines. They may also be employed by companies to deal with all media in advertising (see below), promotion, or public relations work. Different interests can be satisfied, depending upon the work setting. The foods major might work for a food producing company, the clothing major could be employed by a pattern company. College education is necessary.

Advertising Occupations (DOT Code 164.068)

Related to the communications area, the person interested in home economics may also be employed by advertising companies to handle various accounts. Writing ability, creativity, artistic talent, and sales sense may all be helpful to a home economist employed in advertising. College education is necessary.

VISTA

VISTA is a government program designed to utilize volunteer workers in helping disadvantaged people in the United States. Volunteers may work in cities or in rural areas teaching skills or providing services in the areas of cooking, sewing, home management, and money management. No particular training is required, but prior to going to an assignment, training in procedures is provided.

Peace Corps

The Peace Corps is a government organization intended to help people in underdeveloped countries by providing skilled training and services. It is a volunteer service which asks only that interest and ability be demonstrated. Training is similar to VISTA.

Transportation Occupations (DOT Code 352.878, 350.878)

Home economists may be employed by airlines or railroads to perform various services. They may be employed as dietitians or stewards/stewardesses. Airlines use catering services for meals. Railroads may have dining cars which provide meals. Both airlines and railroads may employ stewards or stewardesses who are trained to look after passengers' needs and comforts. Similar positions may be found on cruise ships. Some additional training beyond high school is required and specific training is given prior to employment. Those employed as dietitians are college graduates.

3

Careers Indirectly Related
To Home Economics

Those jobs that are indirectly related to the field of home economics are also important in considering future opportunities for students interested in the field. It is often possible to find work that allows primary and secondary interests to be merged. Indirectly related jobs in this chapter attempt to call attention to these possibilities.

Foods

Kitchen Machine Operator (DOT Code 318.887)

Kitchen machine operators perform several different types of work such as operating dishwashing machines, potato peelers, mixers, cookers, floor scrubbers, and waxers. On-the-job training is sufficient.

Food and Drug Inspector (DOT Code 168.287)

Food and drug inspectors are usually government employees. They inspect establishments where foods, drugs, cosmetics and similar products are processed, packaged, handled or stored and insure that standards of sanitation and purity are being met. They may use sophisticated instruments for tests or may rely on their own senses. On-the-job training is required.

Meat Cutter (DOT Code 316.781)

Meat cutters clean, cut, trim, bone, and grind meat for sale. They not only weigh, package, price, and display the meat but also may help customers select meat. A high school education is preferred with a 2–3 year apprenticeship or on-the-job training. Vocational or post-secondary training is helpful.

Chemist (DOT Code 022.168)

Chemists study a substance's composition and properties and the changes that take place chemically. Their work may include research, analysis, teaching, or sales to industry, research centers, government agencies, or universities. A bachelor's degree is required, with graduate work preferred for jobs in many areas.

Biochemist (DOT Code 041.081)

Biochemists study chemical properties and processes of living organisms. They may work in industry doing research, in universities teaching, or performing related lab work in hospitals and government agencies. A master's degree is required for professional positions and a Ph.D. for most research or teaching positions.

Hotel-Motel Manager (DOT Code 187.168)

The manager is in charge of the whole operation of the hotel or motel which includes coordination of all departments, from housekeeping to the kitchen, in order to insure that patrons are comfortable and satisfied. A college degree in hotel-motel management is most helpful. Many managers however, acquire their positions by working their way up from lower level jobs within the hotel or motel. In addition, some community colleges offer specialized courses in hotel-motel management.

Clothing

Drycleaning or Laundry Worker (DOT Code 362.782)

Drycleaning workers sort and mark garments, remove spots, operate drycleaning equipment, and press and bag garments. Often they make small repairs, such as sewing on missing buttons. A high school diploma is preferred and on-the-job training is provided. Laundry workers weigh bundles, mark and sort clothes, operate washers and dryers, and fold, mend and wrap clothes for the customer. They may assist customers with self-operated machines in a launderette. Eighth-grade education may be sufficient; however, high school education is necessary for supervisory or office jobs. On-the-job training usually is provided.

Upholsterer, Refinisher (DOT Code 730.381, 763.381)

These workers upholster and recondition furniture. They repair springs, frames and damaged parts and replace fabric on the piece. Usually years of on-the-job training are needed to learn the trade, however high school or vocational school classes in woodwork, chair caning, and furniture repair may be helpful. Refinishers repair and recondition wood furniture. They are knowledgeable about kinds of wood and techniques for stripping, staining and finishing wood. Training is similar to that of the upholsterer.

Boutique Owner

The boutique shop which handles clothes and accessories requires the skills of many different people such as a salesperson, a buyer, a display person, and a business detail person. Often these skills are found in one person. A high school education is necessary and some additional training in business is most helpful.

Model (DOT Code 297.868)

Models are used to display clothes in fashion shows, advertising, magazines and displays. A high school diploma is necessary and additional training in "charm" or modeling may be helpful.

Cosmetologist or Beautician (DOT Code 332.271)

Cosmetologists may style hair, give manicures, facials, and apply cosmetics for models, actors or actresses, or private individuals. High school education is helpful but 6 to 12 months of beauty school must be completed and state licensing is required.

Textile Chemist (DOT Code 022.081)

Textile chemists work for textile companies analyzing and developing fibers for fabrics. They may work in research or in development of new or better fibers for textile production. A college degree is necessary.

Quality Control Inspector (DOT Code 019.281)

The person who works as a quality control inspector monitors the quality and consistency of fabrics produced in textile factories. On-the-job training is provided and some production experience is usually required.

Child Development

Toy Designer (DOT Code 142.081)

Toy designers use imagination plus an awareness of children's likes and needs to design toys that are fun, functional, attractive, safe, and sometimes educational. All creations must be able to be produced at competitive prices. High school education plus some post-secondary education is necessary.

Toy Manufacturer (DOT Code 189.118)

Toy manufacturers are business people who manage the toy industry. They take ideas and concepts from designers and decide which ones are to be produced. Manufacturers must have good business sense as well as creativity and experience. Most business people have high school and college education. There is a possibility that high school education plus experience may be sufficient.

Child Psychologist (DOT Code 045.088)

Psychologists study human behavior and child psychologists deal solely with children. Using tests, interviews, case histories and games, the psychologist seeks to understand the child's problems. At least a master's degree is required, often a Ph.D. Most states require special certification.

Child Welfare Worker (DOT Code 195.108)

Working primarily with cases involving children, this type of welfare worker attempts to solve family, social or school problems. Sometimes it is necessary to remove the child from the natural home and find placement in a foster home or institution. A college degree is a minimum requirement and graduate work is required for certification.

Family Health Worker (DOT Code 070.108, 168.168, 075.128)

Usually employed by civic groups or government agencies, the family health worker attempts to educate families in nutritional and economical cooking practices. Many work in urban areas and work with large families. A college degree is required.

Teacher Aide

The basic function of teacher aides is to assist classroom teachers. They perform many non-teaching duties such as collecting and reporting lunch money, preparing audio-visual materials, grading papers, and supervising playgrounds and lunchrooms, as well as some basic teaching duties. Aides often help individual students or small groups of students with special educational problems. While college education is helpful, some aides have experience which substitutes for formal education.

Family Relationships

Adult Education Teacher (DOT Code 099.228)

Adult classes range from non-credit avocational courses such as wood refinishing to courses taken for academic credit, such as law or government. These classes are offered to adults who have left or finished high school and who wish to return. Usually classes are offered after regular school hours and the teacher is certified. There are opportunities for non-certified people to teach special interest classes that do not offer high school credit. The certified teacher is a college graduate.

Social Worker (DOT Code 195.108)

Social work involves alleviating or solving social problems, giving information, arranging assistance in finances, housing, medical services, etc. Workers refer clients to other agencies for further assistance if needed. Social workers are employed in a variety of settings but most are in urban areas. A college degree is required and graduate work is necessary for certification.

Sociologist (DOT Code 054.088)

Sociologists study human social behavior. They may study social phenomena or teach or conduct research in colleges or universities. They may work for the government, research organizations, businesses, or industries. A master's degree is required and often a Ph.D. is necessary.

Geriatrics Worker (DOT Code 195.108)

Working with older people can be done in many different settings. Geriatrics workers are employed in nursing homes, retirement centers, hospitals, community centers, or churches. They may provide activities for the people, teaching crafts or skills, or they may spend time simply talking with the older people about their needs, concerns, and interests. Some geriatrics workers are employed to work with older people in their homes, helping them solve problems related to managing the home. Most people in this field have a high school diploma and some additional training.

Housing

Contract Cleaners

Contract cleaners are people who contract to clean public institutions or private homes. In public places they may be responsible for daily janitorial work as well as periodic thorough cleaning. In private homes the cleaners may contract to do seasonal house cleaning such as washing walls and woodwork, shampooing rugs, and washing windows. High school education may be helpful as well as specific vocational training.

Apartment Manager (DOT Code 186.168)

Apartment managers usually work in houses or complexes. They manage the business of keeping apartments occupied and in good repair. They hear tenants' complaints and suggestions and collect rent. Post-secondary training is necessary.

Furniture Salespeople (DOT Code 274.358)

Salespeople in the furniture field must be knowledgeable about the many kinds of furniture. As in all selling jobs, the salesperson must know the merchandise and be able to describe its strong features to the customer. On-the-job training is given.

Redecorator

A redecorator helps customers decide what changes will be best in a home or an office. After consulting with the client, proposing and discussing various possibilities, the redecorator will develop a decorating plan and supervise the painting, papering, rebuilding and furniture selection. Two or three years training beyond high school is necessary.

Real Estate Agent or Broker (DOT Code 250.358)

Real estate agents rent, buy or sell property for clients on a commission basis. They interview clients who are interested in buying or selling property for information concerning their interests. They provide clients with property information and may arrange to have contracts, deeds, leases, and mortgages drawn up. Short courses are available to help prepare individuals for state board certification examinations.

Moving, Storage Consultant

Moving and storage consultants work with people who need to

move or store possessions. Since many kinds of materials (e.g., furniture, clothes, china) need to be moved or stored, the consultant must have experience with all in order to evaluate the job and discuss methods and costs with the client. Some on-the-job training is given but post-high school training would be helpful.

City Planning Consultant (DOT Code 199.168, 199.388)

City or urban planners prepare long-term plans for urban development. They study population growth and trends, public facilities, land usage, and economics factors, and present plans to civic authorities for action. These people require college training in the field. There are also city planning aides who research much of the material used by city planners. Some post-high school education is needed.

Consumer Education

Banker (DOT Code 186.168)

Banking institutions offer a variety of jobs. Bank officers include the president, vice president, cashier and treasurer. These people are the administrators of the bank and manage loans, trust funds, checking and savings accounts, and investment counseling. A college degree is needed and many banks require a training period in addition. Bank clerks deliver records, handle the checks, deposits and withdrawals, keep accounts, records and files, and do clerical work using typewriters, calculators, and/or other business machines. A high school diploma and on-the-job training are required.

Insurance Agent (DOT Code 250.258)

The field of insurance offers several jobs. Salespeople and counselors are employed by insurance companies to work with prospective clients. These people discuss the clients' insurance needs in terms of house and property, life, car, health, personal insurance. Clerks are employed to answer clients' questions concerning policies. Banks sometimes employ people to work as insurance consultants. College training is preferred but a high school education and experience may be another route. On-the-job training is usually given regardless of education.

Public Relations Worker (DOT Code 165.068)

Public relations people plan and conduct activities and communications that will promote favorable images of the companies they represent. This may be done through television, radio, newspapers, magazines, pamphlets, or speeches. Public relations people collect data for their company, contact people, and arrange special events. A college degree is usually required.

Advertising Specialist (DOT Code 050.088)

Advertising has several jobs in the field. Advertising specialists and advertising aides plan a company's advertising program in which they attempt to promote sales. Working closely with company officials and sales department, they prepare pamphlets for publication, approve layouts and copy, and may prepare sales kits, displays, or outlines. College training is preferred but 2–3 years of post-high school study may also be acceptable. In addition there are advertising copywriters, advertising designers, layout personnel, advertising sales representatives, as well as clerical jobs. With the exception of the advertising designer, the other jobs are fairly well described in previous areas. The advertising designer devises advertising layouts for television, newspapers, magazines, billboards, mail circulars, and posters. High school education is necessary with 2–3 years additional training.

General

Nursing Occupations (DOT Code 079.378, 354.878, 075.128)

Nurses provide care and services to patients in hospitals, nursing homes, private homes, industries, schools, and private or public organizations (e.g., Red Cross, County Health Services). There are several programs of training — 2-year college courses, 3-year nursing schools, 4-year degree college courses. Certification is required and is obtained by passing state board examinations. Practical nurses receive a shorter training, usually 1 year.

Physical Therapist (DOT Code 079.378)

Physical therapists work to rehabilitate patients who have physical disabilities. Disabilities may be caused by muscular, nervous, or bone diseases or injuries. A variety of techniques are used in treatment such as radiation, massage, and exercise. The therapist helps the patient learn to use braces and prosthetic devices. A college degree and certification are necessary.

Occupational Therapist

Occupational therapists work with patients who have mental or physical handicaps in developing educational, occupational or recreational skills. A college degree and clinical training are necessary.

4

Implementing Career Education
in the Home Economics Class

Knowing something about home economics, career education, and jobs directly and indirectly related to home economics is helpful; however, more important is how they are synthesized into a meaningful program for the classroom. There is no one single way to implement career education. What follows is the author's thinking. Each home economics teacher, however, will think of other ways to use the ideas in the classroom.

Sources of Career Information

Resource People

Many resource people are available right in the school. These people can be helpful in planning career education in the classroom. One such person is the counselor. Most counselors will be good resources for finding and ordering relevant materials as well as developing the career education program. Free materials from organizations and companies abound and can be obtained simply by requesting them. Counselors should be able to supply the names of these sources. Films and filmstrips are available. Some may be borrowed, others must be purchased. The Manpower Development and Training Program has some very useful and informative films. Many high school counselors are quite knowledgeable about career development and will have good practical suggestions for the classroom teacher. Discussion with the counselor may be very helpful in determining what to do in relating careers to the subject matter.

In addition to this very accessible person, the state department of education usually has resource people available for use by the school. These people will be found in both the home economics and guidance fields. Because career education has received so much impetus in recent years, there are specialists in career education and these people can be most helpful to the classroom teacher. Some states will have career resource centers located in different geographic areas of the state. These centers are excellent sources not only for all kinds of materials but also for leadership in instigating, implementing and improving career development programs.

Communities offer a variety of help. Inviting speakers to come to the classroom and describe their work, interests, training and to answer students' questions is often valuable. To be successful, this method requires preparing both the speaker and the students. The speaker needs some idea of what information is desired, a time limit for the discussion, and some background related to what students have previously covered. Students need to determine what they desire to know and must be prepared to find out that information. Although inviting speakers to the classroom is an easy thing to do, seeing people in their actual work environment is often much more meaningful. A food processing worker can describe what he or she does on the job, but seeing the production line and the work environment presents quite a different picture. In addition, a worker often feels more comfortable on the job rather than in a formal classroom environment. Field trips, then, are another way to present occupations and workers to students.

Student Projects and Activities

When the whole group cannot view the work setting, there are several other alternatives. One is using a video tape camera and making a video tape of the workers and their work setting. Usually there is a trained person (an audio-visual specialist) available to operate the equipment. Students can prepare interviews with workers and tape the interview as well as some aspects of the work environment. Another possibility is to have students prepare the video tape of the worker without a formal interview, and also prepare a commentary to accompany the tape. If there is a speech-media-communications class in the school, a joint project might be developed. When tapes are completed the project can be shared with others and then stored for future use in other classes.

This same technique can be used with slides. Much less expensive equipment is involved since a relatively inexpensive camera can be used. Students can plan the series and use the camera to take pictures of workers and the work setting. A tape recorder can be used to prepare a tape which carries the commentary for the slide presentation. The 1973 May-June issue of *Illinois Teacher*, a publication of the Division of Home Economics Education, has an excellent article concerning a Michigan project on waitressing as a career. The commentary is presented along with a description of the slides. The November-December issue of that journal for the same year has an article entitled "Career Exploration Via Slides." It discusses jobs related directly and indirectly to home economics.

Tape recordings are another source of information which can be prepared by students. After researching a job, the students may write a script and make the tape. Students may work together and role play the parts on the tape. This method allows other students to hear the information and provides a library of different occupational information prepared by students.

If students are very creative and ambitious, films describing jobs may be made. This is a bit more difficult project and may take some special techniques. Additional help may be needed for this project. While this is more difficult, perhaps, than some techniques, it should be remembered that projects developed and produced by students are often the most worthwhile.

There are other things that students can do themselves, such as conducting interviews and preparing reports on people employed in the community. These are simply reported in oral or written form to the class. Using commercially printed material, the students can report on jobs by describing the job, the training possibilities, the personality traits and interests of persons employed in the job, employment opportunities and future outlook.

Role playing, which allows students to portray different parts in a situation, such as a decorator and customer, helps show the factors that are important for each one. Of course, some information about the job of decorator is necessary prior to the role-playing situation. Students will find that information in several different places — the school guidance office, library, or in the community.

Printed Material

There is a wealth of printed career information material available. As mentioned before, organizations and companies will send pamphlets, often in quantities, free of charge. Many of these sources are listed in Appendix A. In addition to free material there are several commercial sources that provide a systematic presentation of material on many occupations. These are sources such as Chronicle Guidance Publications, Science Research Associates, Careers, and Occupational Awareness. (See Appendix B for addresses.) These companies publish series of pamphlets which present information such as job description, working conditions, personal qualities, training needed, earnings, and the future employment outlook.

The *Occupational Outlook Handbook* provides much the same kind of information on selected occupations and the *Dictionary of Occupational Titles* gives much job information. All these sources are valuable for the student who reads extensively, however other ways of gathering information must be found for those with limited reading skills.

Films, Filmstrips, and Games

Many educational companies have developed career education programs which include printed material but also include cassettes or tapes that describe jobs. Some are presented as worker interviews, but most are presented simply as an employed person describing his or her job. Filmstrips are available which provide much the same information. The obvious advantage of filmstrips is that for some students the visual presentation will help in keeping their attention and facilitate understanding. Filmstrips can be used with a whole class, by a group of interested students, or by an individual student using a small viewer and a tape or record player. Some available filmstrips are listed in the resource appendix.

Films are produced by many different sources. Some may be obtained free, some may be rented at nominal fees, others must be purchased. It probably is not practical to buy many films because they become obsolete in a rather short time. Rental may be a better option, however sometimes films do not arrive when desired, neither are they available on short notice. The same problems can exist when films are borrowed from agencies, but many good films are available and this source should not be discarded because of the problems.

Career games are games which set up situations and limitations similar to those one might encounter in daily living and allow players to make decisions and see the consequences that follow. Games can provide ideas and alternatives in a non-threatening environment without risking potentially damaging experiences. There are games which can be developed in the classroom concerning job opportunities, job interviewing, job seeking. One such example can be found in the November-December (1973) issue of *Illinois Teacher*. This game, which deals with seeking job employment, was devised by a high school home economics teacher. Other games will be invented by students and teachers themselves.

Work-Study

Work-study programs offer another means to relate education and occupations meaningfully. Work-study provides students, usually juniors and seniors, with the opportunity to go to school one half-day and work the other half. Coordinators for the program work in a classroom setting with students discussing work values, on-the-job problems, unions, apprenticeships, further training, retirement, social security — all those things that relate work to formal class work. Coordinators also visit with the work supervisor to discuss the students' performance on the job. The fundamental purpose of work-study programs is to provide students with on-the-job experience in areas they might want to pursue after leaving school. Work-study programs also tend to be a means of retaining students in school. Homemaking jobs using work-study include those that deal with food (cook, waitress, waiter), clothing (fabric departments, stores, drycleaning, laundering), service to persons (nursing homes, child care centers, nursery schools), home furnishing (furniture stores, paint and paper stores), and institutional and home management (hotel-motels, restaurants).

School and Community Resources

Many students work, and these youngsters should be used as sources of career information. They can describe quite clearly and accurately what they do, what they like and dislike about the work, what others around them do and what kind of training is needed.

People and place resources in the community should not be overlooked. Surveys of the local work settings and those related to home economics, such as welfare offices, banks, insurance companies, nursing-convalescent centers, hospitals, child care centers, nursery schools, retail stores, restaurants, motels, hotels, extension services, county regional planning offices, and zoning offices, should be conducted. Parents, grandparents, older brothers and sisters of students, employment workers who know about local and regional employment conditions and employment trends, school personnel such as cafeteria workers and school social worker, as well as local business people can be identified for use as resource people in the classroom. Clubs such as Business and Professional Women, Kiwanis, Lions, Rotary or the Chamber of Commerce can help provide lists of people in many home economics-related areas.

Computerized Information

Gaining increased popularity are computer systems which may serve as a help for students obtaining career information. The computer can store and retrieve much information. If it is so programmed it can provide the student with much information concerning work relative to his or her interests. While these systems are often expensive, they are an extremely versatile and attractive career information source.

Future Homemakers of America

Future Homemakers of America, the vocational-educational youth organization for home economics students, offers another avenue which may be used in career development. The emphasis of the FHA program is to encourage youth to discover their concerns and then proceed to some action. If the local FHA chapter identifies career choice as a concern area, this becomes another opportunity to relate home economics careers to home economics interests.

The Career Development Approach

The challenge for the classroom teacher is to relate subject matter to careers in order to increase its relevancy to the student. How one does this varies with the individual. Being creative may help, but interest and involvement, coupled with a dedication to career development concepts, are equally important. There are an infinite number of ways to bring career development into any subject area, but commitment and planning are essential. Not every student will be "turned on" by a career education program but not every student is "turned on" by the present curriculum either. The promise of a career education approach is that it can involve students in a way which encourages them to relate what they are learning in school to what's going on "outside" and therefore to what they need in the future. It allows teachers to involve resources other than just themselves and shares the educational growth of students with others.

Resources and Their Addresses

Advertising

American Association of
Advertising Agencies
200 Park Avenue
New York, New York 10017

Advertising and Communications

Fashion Institute of Technology
227 West 27 Street
New York, New York 10001

Agriculture

U.S. Department of Agriculture
Washington, D.C. 20250

Airlines

Air Transport Association of
America
1709 New York Avenue, NW
Washington, D.C. 20006

Braniff Education Systems, Inc.
Post Office Box 35001
Dallas, Texas 75235

United Airlines, Inc.
Stewardess Recruitment Section
Post Office Box 66140
Chicago, Illinois 60666

American Red Cross

American National Red Cross
Office of Personnel
17th and D Streets
Washington, D.C. 20006

Apprenticeship

Bureau of Apprenticeship &
Training

Apprenticeship (cont'd.)

U.S. Department of Labor
Main Labor Building
Washington, D.C. 20210

Art

Philadelphia College of Art
Broad and Pine Streets
Philadelphia, Pennsylvania
19102

Baking Industry

American Bakers Association
1700 Pennsylvania Avenue, NW
Washington, D.C. 20006

Banking

The American Bankers
Association
1120 Connecticut Avenue, NW
Washington, D.C. 20036

Mortgage Bankers Association of
America
1125 15th Street, NW
Washington, D.C. 20005

Beauty

National Beauty Career Center
3839 White Plains Road
Bronx, New York 10467

Boys Club

Recruitment and Placement
Service
Boys Club of America
771 First Avenue
New York, New York 10017

Boy Scouts

Boy Scouts of America
Personnel Service
North Brunswick, New Jersey
08902

Builders

Associated Builders &
Contractors, Inc.
Post Office Box 698
Glen Burnee, Maryland 21061

National Association of Home
Builders
1625 L Street, NW
Washington, D.C. 20036

Business

Administration Management
Society
Publications Department
Willow Grove, Pennsylvania
19090

American Society of Association
Executives
2000 K Street, NW
Washington, D.C. 20006

Camp Fire Girls

Camp Fire Girls, Inc.
1740 Broadway
New York, New York 10019

Chefs

Culinary Institute of America,
Inc.
393 Prospect Street, NW
New Haven, Connecticut 06511

Educational Director
National Restaurant Association
153 North Lake Shore Drive
Chicago, Illinois 60610

The Education Institute
American Hotel and Motel
Association
Kellogg Center
Michigan State University
East Lansing, Michigan 48823

Chemistry

American Chemical Society
Educational Activities
Department
1155 16th Street, NW
Washington, D.C. 20036

Church

National Council of the Churches
of Christ in USA
Department of Ministry
Church Occupations
475 Riverside Drive, Room 760
New York, New York 10027

Club Management

Club Managers Association of
America
5530 Wisconsin Avenue, Suite
705
Washington, D.C. 20015

Community Organizations

United Way of America
801 North Fairfax Street
Alexandria, Virginia 22314

Cosmetology

Cosmetology Accrediting
Commission
1601 18th Street, NW
Washington, D.C. 20009

Dairy and Food Industries

Purdue University
Food Sciences Institute
104 Smith Hall
Lafayette, Indiana 47907

Dietetics

The American Dietetic
Association
620 North Michigan Avenue
Chicago, Illinois 60611

Drycleaning

The Registrar
International Fabricare Institute

Drycleaning (cont'd.)

909 Burlington Avenue
Silver Spring, Maryland 20910

Education

National Center for Information
on Careers in Education
1607 New Hampshire Avenue,
NW
Washington, D.C. 20009

Fashion

Fashion Institute of Technology
227 West 27 Street
New York, New York 10001

Federal Civil Service

Job Information Center
Washington Area Office
U.S. Civil Service Commission
Washington, D.C. 20415

Food and Nutrition

Food and Nutrition Service
U.S. Department of Agriculture
Washington, D.C. 20250

American Institute of Nutrition
9650 Wisconsin Avenue, NW
Washington, D.C. 20006

Public Relations Department
Rochester Institute of
Technology
65 Plymouth Avenue
Rochester, New York 14608

Food Chain Retailing

National Association of Food
Chains
1725 Eye Street, NW
Washington, D.C. 20006

Food Inspection

Animal and Plant Health
Inspection Service
U.S. Department of Agriculture
Washington, D.C. 20250

Food Science

Food Service Careers
Institute for the Food Service
Industry
120 South Riverside Plaza
Chicago, Illinois 60606

The Institute of Nutrition and
Food Technology
Ohio State University
1615 Neil Avenue
Columbus, Ohio 43210

Food Science Institute
Smith Hall
Purdue University
Lafayette, Indiana 47907

Institute of Food Technologists
Scholarship Center
221 North LaSalle Street
Chicago, Illinois 60601

Girl Scouts

Girl Scouts of USA
830 Third Avenue
New York, New York 10022

Grocers

National Association of Retail
Grocers
360 North Michigan Avenue
Chicago, Illinois 60601

Home Economics

American Home Economics
Association
2010 Massachusetts Avenue, NW
Washington, D.C. 20036

Hospitals

Hospital Financial Management
Association
840 North Lake Shore Drive
Chicago, Illinois 60611

American Hospital Association
840 North Lake Shore Drive
Chicago, Illinois 60611

Hospitals (cont'd.)

American College of Hospital
Administrators
840 North Lake Shore Drive
Chicago, Illinois 60611

Hotel

Council on Hotel, Restaurant &
Institutional Education
1522 K Street, NW
Washington, D.C. 20005

Housekeeping

The National Executive
Housekeeping Association, Inc.
Business and Professional
Building
Second Avenue
Gallipolis, Ohio 45631

Insurance

Insurance Information Institute
110 Williams Street
New York, New York 10038

Investment Council Association
of America, Inc.
127 East 59th Street
New York, New York 10022

Interior Design

American Institute of Interior
Design
673 5th Avenue
New York, New York 10022

National Society of Interior
Designers, Inc.
157 West 57th Street, Suite 700
New York, New York 10019

Journalism

Sigma Delta Chi
Professional Journalistic Society
35 Wacker Drive
Chicago, Illinois 60601

The Newspaper Fund, Inc.
Post Office Box 300
Princeton, New Jersey 08540

Marketing

Sales and Marketing Executives
International
Career Education Division
630 Third Avenue
New York, New York 10017

American Marketing Association
222 South Riverside Plaza
Chicago, Illinois 60606

National Consumer Finance
Association
Educational Services Division
1000 16th Street, NW
Washington, D.C. 20036

Meat Industry

Department of Personnel
Relations
American Meat Institute
56 East Van Buren Street
Chicago, Illinois 60605

Mental Health

National Association for Mental
Health
10 Columbus Circle
New York, New York 10019

Motel

Educational Institute of the
American Hotel and Motel
Association
77 Kellogg Center
East Lansing, Michigan 48823

Nursing

National Association for Practical
Nursing
Education and Service, Inc.
122 East 42nd Street
New York, New York 10017

American Nurses' Association
2420 Pershing Road
Kansas City, Missouri 64108

Occupational Therapy

American Occupational Therapy
Assoc.

Occupational Therapy (cont'd.)

6000 Executive Blvd.
Suite 200
Rockville, Maryland 20852

Psychology

American Psychological
Association
1200 17th Street, NW
Washington, D.C. 20036

Public Health

Society for Public Health
Education, Inc.
655 Sutter Street, Suite 408
San Francisco, California 94102

Public Relations

Career Information Service
Public Relations Society of
America
845 Third Avenue
New York, New York 10022

Purchasing Management

National Association of
Purchasing Management
11 Park Place
New York, New York 10007

Real Estate

Department of Education
National Assoc. of Real Estate
Boards
155 East Superior Street
Chicago, Illinois 60611

Restaurant

Council of Hotel, Restaurant, and
Institutional Education
1522 K Street, NW
Washington, D.C. 20005

Retailing

Ohio State Council of Retail
Merchants

Retailing (cont'd.)

71 East State Street
Columbus, Ohio 43215

Rural Electrification

Rural Electrification
Administration
U.S. Department of Agriculture
Washington, D.C. 20250

Sales and Marketing

Sales and Marketing Executives
International
Career Education Department
630 Third Avenue
New York, New York 10017

Social Work

Social Work Career Information
Service
National Association of Social
Workers
600 Southern Building
15th and H Streets, NW
Washington, D.C. 20005

Textile

Fashion Institute of Technology
227 West 27th Street
New York, New York 10001

Publishers of Commercial Materials

Careers
Largo, Florida 33540

Chronicle Guidance Publications, Inc.
Moravia, New York 13118

Occupational Awareness
Box 5098
Los Angeles, California 90055

Science Research Associates, Inc.
259 East Erie Street
Chicago, Illinois 60611

Filmstrips, Films, Games, Pamphlets, Books, and Magazines

Filmstrips

Educational Dimensions Corporation
Box 126
Stamford, Connecticut 06901

Art Careers in Advertising
Careers in Illustration
Writing Careers in Advertising
Careers in Fashion Design
Graphic Careers in Advertising
Careers in Interior Design

Guidance Associates
41 Washington Avenue
Pleasantville, New York 10570

People Who Make Things
People Who Influence Others
People Who Create Art
People Who Organize Facts
People Who Work in Science
People Who Help Others
Jobs for You: It's Happening in Home Economics

Pathescope Educational Films, Inc.
71 Weyman Avenue
New Rochelle, New York 10802

Careers in Health Services
Careers in Journalism
Careers in Business Administration
Careers in Sales

Filmstrips (cont'd.)

Careers in Food Service
Careers in Graphic Arts
Careers in Fashion and Textiles
Careers in Social Work

Singer Education and Training Products
Society for Visual Education, Inc.
1345 Diversey Parkway
Chicago, Illinois 60614

Job Opportunities in a Supermarket
Job Opportunities in a Restaurant

Films

Newist-Vocational Guidance Division
787 Lombardi Avenue
Post Office Box 7711
Green Bay, Wisconsin 54303

Food Distribution Occupations

Milady Publishing Corporation
3839 White Plains Road
Bronx, New York 10467

Fashion Merchandising As Your Career

National Audiovisual Center
National Archives and Records Service
General Services Administration
Washington, D.C. 20409

Cooks and Chefs
Opportunities in Sales and Merchandising
Opportunities in Hotels and Motels
Jobs in Cosmetology
Jobs in Baking

(These are Manpower Films from the U.S. Department of Labor)

Aims Instructional Media Services, Inc.
Post Office Box 1010
Hollywood, California 90028

Is A Career in the Hotel or Motel Business for You?
Is A Career in Finance, Insurance or Real Estate for You?

These may be ordered from Counselor Films, Inc.
1728 Cherry Street
Philadelphia, Pennsylvania 19103

Films (cont'd.)

Butterick Fashion Marketing Company
Post Office Box 1945
Altoona, Pennsylvania 16603

Careers in the Fashion Industry

Games

Educational Development Corporation
Post Office Box 45663
Tulsa, Oklahoma 74145

Career Development Laboratory
Career Games

Parker Bros.
Salem, Massachusetts

Careers

Western Publishing Company
New York, New York

Life Career

Pamphlets

King Features
235 East 45th Street
New York, New York 10017

Series arranged by 15 career clusters presented in comic book form.

Consumer and Homemaking Related Careers

Associated Publishers' Guidance Publications Center
355 State Street
Los Altos, California 94022

Looking Forward to a Career Series
Home Economics

Career Monographs on Opportunity Occupations

Cook-Chef
Cosmetology
Hotel-Motel Maid
Physical Therapy
Licensed Practical Nurse
Professional Nursing
Waiter-Waitress

Pamphlets (cont'd.)

American Home Economics Association
2010 Massachusetts Avenue
Washington, D.C. 20036

> Career Packet
> The Wonderful World of Home Economics
> A Career With a Future
> Home Economics Careers

Books

Associated Publishers' Guidance Publication Center
335 State Street
Los Altos, California 94022

> *Food Preparation*, Rosenthal and Folsom
> *Food Science and Technology*, Endres
> *Hotel-Motel Industry*, Henkin
> *Industrial Design*, Pulos
> *Interior Design and Decoration*, Ball
> *Market Research*, Plattens

Richards Rosen Press, Inc.
New York, New York 10010

> Careers in Depth Series

>> *Your Future as an Airline Steward/Stewardess*, Randell
>> *Banking*, Boynton
>> *Beauty Business*, Fashion Group
>> *Beauty Culture*, Gelb
>> *Dietitian*, American Dietetic Association
>> *Fashion Design*, Fashion Group
>> *Home Economist*, Paris
>> *Hotel Management*, Sonnabend
>> *Interior Design*, Greer
>> *Model*, Mac Gil

Vocational Guidance Manuals
235 East 45 Street
New York, New York 10017

> *The Hotel Industry*
> *Textile Careers*
> *Food Preparation*

Superintendent of Documents
U.S. Government Printing Office
Washington, D.C. 20402

> *Occupational Outlook Handbook, 1973–74 Edition*
> *Dictionary of Occupational Titles*

Magazines

Forecast for Home Economics
2280 Arbor Blvd.
Dayton, Ohio 45439

Journal of Home Economics
2010 Massachusetts Avenue NW
Washington, D.C. 20036

What's New in Home Economics
666 5th Avenue
New York, New York 10019

BIBLIOGRAPHY

Baldwin, K. E. *The AHEA saga.* Washington, D.C.: American Home Economics Association, 1949.

Bartolomeo, M. Career discovery: Opportunities in health service. *Forecast for Home Economics,* 1973, *19:1,* pp. 147–148.

Bartolomeo, M. Career discovery: Opportunities in science and technology. *Forecast for Home Economics,* 1973, *19:3,* pp. 42–44.

Bartolomeo, M. Career discovery: Opportunities in selling. *Forecast for Home Economics,* 1973, *19:4,* pp. 24–26.

Bartolomeo, M. Career discovery: Opportunities in law enforcement. *Forecast for Home Economics,* 1974, *19:6,* pp. 55–56.

Creating careers in home economics. *Forecast for Home Economics,* 1972, *18:1,* pp. 68–69; 1970, p. 172.

Ellard, M. Wanted: One waitress. *Illinois Teacher,* 1973, *16:5,* pp. 375–381.

Focus on . . . careers in extension. *What's New in Home Economics,* 1974, *38:2,* pp. 6–7.

Focus on . . . men in home economics. *What's New in Home Economics,* 1974, *38:3,* pp. 34–36.

Handbook of job facts. Chicago: Science Research Associates, 1972.

Hoyt, K. B., Evans, R. N., Mackin, E. F., & Mangum, S. L. *Career education: What it is and how to do it.* Salt Lake City: Olympus, 1972.

Hoyt, K. B., & Woalard, S. S. *High school curriculum guide.* Center for Occupational Education, 1973.

Huetle, K. Highway to job success — a game. *Illinois Teacher,* 1973, *17:2,* pp. 98–107.

Ideas for teaching boys. *Forecast for Home Economics,* 1973, *19:3,* pp. 20–23.

Jobs in consumer and homemaking education. Chicago: Science Research Associates, 1973.

McConnell, E. The history of home economics, part 1. *Forecast for Home Economics,* 1970, *16:1,* pp. 86–87, 134.

McConnell, E. The history of home economics, part 2. *Forecast for Home Economics,* 1970, *16:2,* pp. 58–59, 89.

McConnell, E. Trudy Lieberman: A voice for consumer rights. *Forecast for Home Economics*, 1971, *16:8*, pp. 24, 26.

Myhra, C. Career exploration via slides. *Illinois Teacher*, 1973, *17:2*, pp. 108–115.

Reel, M. Relating FHA to the Classroom. *Journal of Home Economics*, 1974, *66:2*, pp. 19–22.

Terrass, J. J. Let's get going with occupational home economics! *Journal of Home Economics*, 1974, *66:2*, pp. 23–24.

U.S. Department of Labor. *Dictionary of occupational titles*, vol. 1, 1965.

U.S. Department of Labor. *Occupational outlook handbook*, Why a special issue on teaching boys? *Forecast for Home Economics*, 1973, *19:3*, p. 17.

INDEX

Adult education teacher, 6
Advertising occupations, 28, 37
AHEA, 6
Alterations, 17
Apartment manager, 35
Apparel presser, 17
Atwater, H., 7
Babysitter, 19
Baker, 15
Bane, L., 7
Banker, 36
Beautician, 32
Beecher, C. E., 2
Bevier, I., 7
Biochemist, 31
Blunt, K., 7
Boutique, owner, 32
Brown, M., 8
Building consultant, 25
Busboy, 14
Busgirl, 14
Business occupations, 16
Buyer, 18, 23
Career information sources, 36–43
Case worker, 22
Chemist, 31
Child psychologist, 33
Child welfare worker, 33
City planning consultant, 36
Classes, 7
Communication occupations, 28
Community resources, 42
Company representatives, 18
Computerized information, 43
Consultant, 27
Consumer advisor, 27
Contract cleaners, 35
Corson, J., 2
Cosmetologist, 32
Count Rumford, 1
Curricular areas, 9–10
    boys' classes, 10
    child care & development, 9, 19–21,
       33–34

clothing, 9, 16–19, 31–32
consumer education, 10, 26–27,
    36–37
family living, 10, 21–23, 34
foods, 9, 13–16, 30–31
housing, 10, 23–26, 35–36
Day care center worker, 20
Dietitian, 15
Dish carrier, 15
Display designer, 19
Domestic Receipt Book, 2
Drapery maker, 17
Dressmaker, 17
Drycleaning worker, 31
Educational relations worker, 22
Emergency Act of 1933, 8
Equipment development occupations,
    25
Equipment salesperson, 25
Extension workers, 28
    child development, 20
    family relationships, 23
    housing, 26
Fabric designer, 18
Fabric salesperson, 18
Family counselor, 23
Family financial counselor, 23
Family health worker, 33
Fashion coordinator, 18
Fashion designer, 19
Fashion illustrator, 19
Films, filmstrips, 41
Food & drug inspector, 30
Food processing worker, 14
Food salesperson, 15
Food scientist, 16
Food service worker, 14
Food technician, 14
Food technologist, 16
Foster parent, 19
Four-H leader, 20
Furniture designer, 24
Furniture salesperson, 35
Future Homemakers of America, 43